**350**

# MARGATE
# & RAMSGATE
# TRAMWAYS

## Robert J Harley

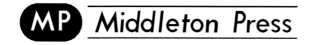
**MP** Middleton Press

*Cover Picture: The Isle of Thanet Tramways catered for crowds of holidaymakers who regularly visited the resorts of Margate, Broadstairs and Ramsgate. Car 54 is depicted at the corner of Athelstan Road, Cliftonville. The tram is packed and will probably remain so until Ramsgate Harbour is reached. (FJ)*

*Cover Colours: These are similar to the red and white livery of the tramcars.*

*Published to mark the centenary of the construction of the tramways.*

*Published January 2001*

*ISBN 1 901706 52 4*

*© Middleton Press, 2000*

*Design Deborah Esher*
*David Pede*

*Published by*
*Middleton Press*
*Easebourne Lane*
*Midhurst, West Sussex*
*GU29 9AZ*
*Tel: 01730 813169*
*Fax: 01730 812601*

*Printed & bound by Biddles Ltd,*
*Guildford and Kings Lynn*

# CONTENTS

# INTRODUCTION AND ACKNOWLEDGEMENTS

In an age when many British cities are rediscovering the value of electric tramways, a true historical perspective can be gained by celebrating the achievements of past pioneers of this form of environmentally friendly transport. This volume serves as a reminder of the centenary of the construction and opening of the Isle of Thanet tramway system. In many respects the "Golden Era" of Thanet was played out to the accompaniment of the trim crimson and cream tramcars which once formed the backbone of local transport.

The present book follows on from my previous work entitled *Thanet's Tramways*, which was published in 1993 and is now out of print. I wish to acknowledge all those who helped with the preparation of the first book, in particular: B.Boddy, C.Carter, D.G.Collyer, R.Elliott, G.Gundry, W.J.Haynes, J.Hiscott, C.M.Jackson, H.J.Paterson Rutherford, E.Shields, R.Thacker, P.Ward, G.Wilton, and L.T.Woodruff. In *Margate and Ramsgate Tramways* the main contributor has been B.J. "Curly" Cross who has generously given his permission for the use of photos from the collection of the late Frank (D.W.K.) Jones (marked FJ in the photo credits). I am also indebted to Dave Jones of the LCC Tramways Trust who now produces prints from the original negatives acquired by B.J.Cross. I wish to record my thanks to the late Sara Leitch, daughter of Dr.Hugh Nicol. Mrs.Leitch was a staunch supporter of the *Tramway Classics* series and hoped that her father's visit on 9th December 1928 would gain a wider audience.

I have tried to acknowledge individual photographers, but inevitably the provenance of some views is unknown or in doubt. No credit after the caption indicates that the picture comes from the author's collection. I tender my apologies to anyone who has been inadvertently omitted from this list of acknowledgements.

# GEOGRAPHICAL SETTING

The Isle of Thanet, as its name suggests, was once entirely separate from the English mainland, but over the centuries the actions of wind, weather and tides have eroded this isolation. Thanet now forms a promontory of the county of Kent at the confluence of the English Channel and the North Sea. Chalk cliffs rise steeply along many parts of the coast, and some of the roads used by the tramways contain appreciable gradients. The soil is very fertile and cornfields were once a common sight on the journey between the three main towns. Ordnance survey maps used in this book are to a scale of 1:2500 and are taken from the 1907 and 1933 editions for the area.

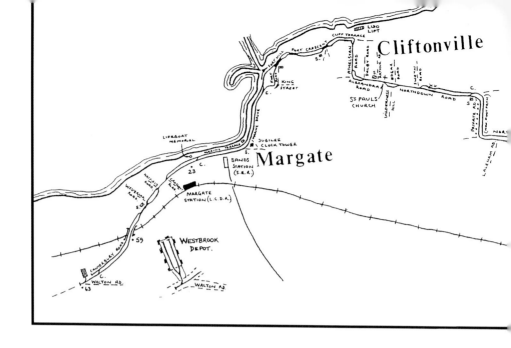

# HISTORICAL BACKGROUND

In 1899 construction started on the Isle of Thanet Tramways and the route from Westbrook to Ramsgate was opened throughout on 6th July 1901. The track gauge was set at 3 ft. 6ins./ 1067mm and double track was laid in anticipation of heavy holiday traffic generated by the many visitors to the seaside resorts. After some initial teething troubles, which saw the new eight wheel tramcars shortened and put on four wheel trucks, the system settled down to a profitable existence. This status was aided by the fact that the tramway company also supplied light and power to the local population. The official title of the undertaking was the Isle of Thanet Electric Tramways and Lighting Company. This was changed in 1924 to the Isle of Thanet Electric Supply Company.

In 1913 the company instituted its first motor bus services which served basically as feeders to the trams. At this time a record number of people were being transported and on warm summer days the eleven miles of route saw the whole fleet of sixty cars in operation crewed by every available employee, including depot fitters, overhead linesmen and permanent way staff. The First World War started in August 1914 and had an immediate effect on passenger and fleet maintenance levels, so that, by November 1918, the cars and track were in poor condition. The company set about putting matters in order and during the post war years instituted a programme of car rebuilding which continued until just before abandonment. The general design of the single truck cars remained traditional and no attempt was made, save for the single deck, one man operated, conversion of car 45, to modernise the fleet by the introduction of top covered trams. Track and overhead also received attention and many roads were repaved as new housing appeared along the route.

The demise of the system was partly as a result of pressure from local councils who felt that the electric supply part of the business was being used to subsidise the trams, thus creating higher bills for consumers. The final nail in the coffin was the receipt of an offer from the East Kent Roadcar Company to run replacement buses. In October 1936 the ITES motor buses passed to East Kent control and on Wednesday, 24th March 1937, car 20 closed the tramway. A unique and efficient system had been lost forever.

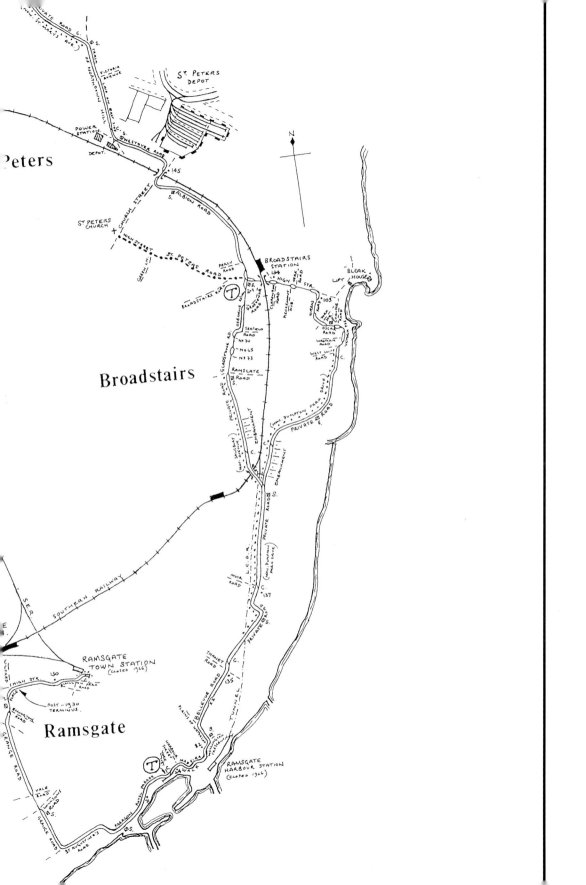

# WESTBROOK TO MARGATE

1.     Car 10 waits at the end of the line in Canterbury Road. It is worth noting in this mid-1930s view that this tram is still maintained in excellent condition, even though it is nearing the end of its operational life. (R.Elliott)

2.     At the same location as the previous picture, car 4 stands empty whilst the motorman and conductor are probably seated in the lower saloon. New housing has already appeared on the corner of Walton Road.

3.     The conductor of an unidentified car of the 51-60 batch glances at the photographer, before the tram pulls away in the direction of Margate. The couple in the lower saloon can avail themselves of the tenpence return fare to Ramsgate. On the left of the picture is the small stabling shed, which did duty as Westbrook Depot. This building still exists and contains its original track layout. (H.Nicol/National Tramway Museum)

4.      We look along Canterbury Road towards Margate after the carriageway had been widened and the original bracket arms had been replaced by span wire construction. In the distance is the tower of All Saints Church.  (FJ)

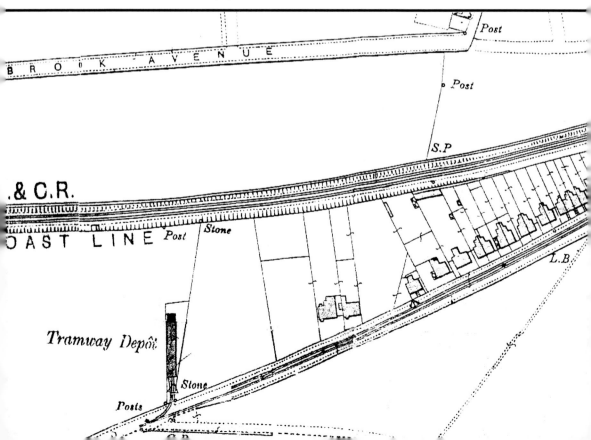

BROOK AVENUE

Post

Post

.& C.R.

S.P

OAST LINE   Post   Stone

L.B

Tramway Depôt

Stone

Posts

5.     Car 26 sits at the back of a three tram convoy. Since the demise of the trams, this area has become thoroughly "suburban" in character, and the cornfields of the 1920s are now a distant memory. (FJ)

6.     We now arrive at the corner of Canterbury Road and All Saints Avenue. Behind car 13 the road rises to cross the bridge over the former South-Eastern & Chatham Railway Kent Coast line. The local steam railways suffered a drop in passengers after the 1901 opening of the tramways. Local folk preferred the convenience of street based public transport.   (FJ)

7.　　Shortly before encountering Margate Seafront, the tramway passed by the Nayland Rock Hotel. Car 28 is pictured in this pre First World War scene.

8.　　Well dressed visitors enjoying the sea air seem to mirror the essence of an Edwardian high summer. In the background we catch sight of car 6, which is working the "Harbours" route (Margate to Ramsgate Harbour), as it prepares to reverse on the nearby crossover.

9.      Time moves on to the 1920s. Car 3 empties before it returns to Ramsgate. It is worth recording that the site to the right of the tram was once the location of Margate Sands Station, which used to generate some short distance local traffic for the tramways.  (FJ)

10.     Above ground level we gain a splendid vista of the seafront. In the centre of the picture are the gardens by Buenos Ayres, whilst, to the left, car 23 proceeds to Westbrook.

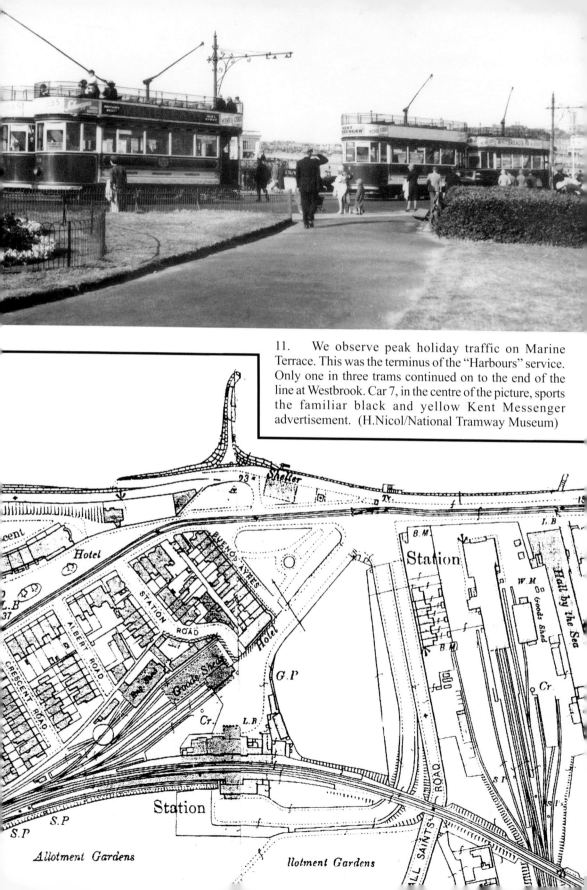

11.    We observe peak holiday traffic on Marine Terrace. This was the terminus of the "Harbours" service. Only one in three trams continued on to the end of the line at Westbrook. Car 7, in the centre of the picture, sports the familiar black and yellow Kent Messenger advertisement. (H.Nicol/National Tramway Museum)

12.    The motorman of car 3 turns round momentarily to check on the situation in the lower saloon. A good working relationship between driver and conductor was vital for the efficient running of the tramway. Sometimes when the conductor was stationed on the top deck and could not easily descend the stairs because of the number of passengers, the driver would open the lower deck bulkhead doors and give assistance to those who wished to alight. Here at the Marine Terrace stop in high season this kind of help was most appreciated.   (M.J.O'Connor/National Tramway Museum)

13.    The Jubilee Clock of 1887 shows 10.55am as cars 24 and 7 inch past the elegant centre poles, which support the overhead wires. This postcard view was sent on 20th August 1906 and it depicts a scene totally devoid of other motorised traffic. Noteworthy vehicles, aside from the trams, are the goat cart, sundry open carriages and bath chairs for invalids and the infirm.

15.    The Edwardian era ushered in an age of elegance for the resorts on the Thanet coast. Holiday visitors just after the turn of the twentieth century seem to have taken a particular pride in their appearance – smartness was the order of the day! In the background is one of the former eight wheel, bogie cars which has how been shortened and placed on a single, four wheel truck.

14.    We remain in the first decade of the twentieth century, as we observe car 28 gently taking the curve from Marine Drive into Marine Terrace.

**37S 8984**

| UP | FARE | DOWN |
|---|---|---|
| 1 | **1D** | 16 |
| 2 | | 15 |
| 3 | | 14 |
| 4 | | 13 |
| 5 | | 12 |
| 6 | | 11 |
| 7 | | 10 |
| 8 | | 9 |
| 9 | | 8 |
| 10 | | 7 |
| 11 | | 6 |
| 12 | | 5 |
| 13 | | 4 |
| 14 | | 3 |
| 15 | | 2 |
| 16 | | 1 |

For Stage Numbers See Fare Bills.

TICKET TO BE SHOWN ON DEMAND.

For Stage Numbers See Fare Bills.

Bell Punch Co. Uxbridge. 11-71

16. Fashions change as we progress to the 1930s. The town of Margate is still as popular as ever and at ten o'clock on a summer's morning the tram in the centre takes on passengers for the ride over to Broadstairs and Ramsgate.

17.   The Promenade and Harbour, Margate is
captured on film some time in the 1920s. The
side bracket arms with their delicate wrought iron
tracery work were erected to replace the original
centre poles at this location. It would seem that
too many early motorists felt an irresistible urge
to collide with the centre poles, therefore the
council asked the tramways company to remove
these potential obstructions from the middle of
the highway. Car 32 approaches the
photographer. In the background one can just
make out the travelling crane on the harbour pier.

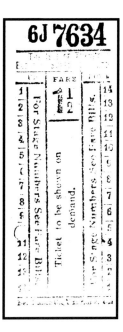

18.    At the corner of Marine Drive and Market Street the double track used by the trams was laid in such a fashion that no two tramcars could pass. To the right of car 1 is one of the tramway company's open top buses on service 1 to Birchington. The date is 9th December 1928. (H.Nicol/National Tramway Museum)

20.    This is the same location as in the previous two photos. Car 3, looking somewhat worse for wear after a period of reduced maintenance enforced by conditions during the First World War, heads along The Parade. By the Albion Hotel at the corner of King Street, the tracks divided – Ramsgate bound trams ascended the gradient of Paradise Street, whilst Margate bound cars descended Fort Road and King Street. (FJ)

19.    Eight wheel car 39 passes the competing wagonettes in this view taken shortly after the tramway opened in July 1901.

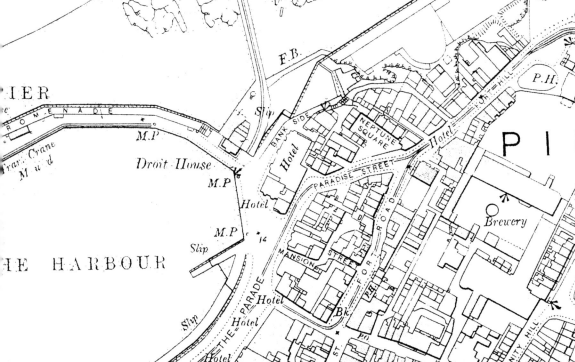

◄────────

21.     One can almost hear the motors of car 12 straining to maintain momentum on the grade up Paradise Street. The conductor, oblivious to the trials of his motorman colleague, is busy collecting fares on the top deck. (C.Carter)

22.     Car 30 climbs onwards – it has reached Neptune Square by Paradise Street. This scene belongs firmly to the past, as a new dual carriageway road now sweeps through the area and the delights of the Paradise Hill Café, with its Luncheon & Tea Rooms, are but a distant memory. (FJ)

23.    Fort Road near Mansion Street, and car
34 descends before coming to a halt at the right
angle bend leading to King Street. (C.Carter)

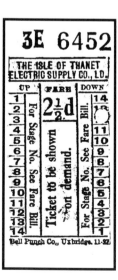

# CLIFTONVILLE
# TO NORTHDOWN

24.    In pristine condition, car 37 looks good for many more years of service. It has just made the ascent to Cliftonville.  (FJ)

25.    Car 32 is depicted on Fort Crescent just past the interlaced track in the foreground. The tram has the original metal destination indicator affixed just below the fleet number. As delivered, all vehicles had their headlamps positioned on the top deck canopy bend. By 1922 all Thanet trams had had the headlamp removed to the dash.

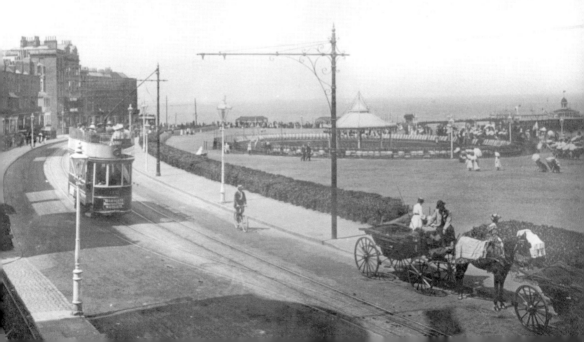

26.     We look eastwards to Fort Paragon. The driver of car 23 has already lowered his right hand window in order to increase the ventilation on this warm summer's day.

## Isle of Thanet Electric Tramways.

### Main Line Service, Ramsgate & Margate, *via* Broadstairs Front.

| | A | A | A | A | B | B | B | B | | | | | | | | | | |
|---|---|---|---|---|---|---|---|---|---|---|---|---|---|---|---|---|---|---|
| Ramsgate S. E. Station | .... | .... | .... | .... | .... | 9 5 | .... | 9 45 | .... | 10 20 | 10 45 | 11 0 | | 5 20 | 5 40 | 6 0 | .... | 6 20 |
| Ramsgate Harbour | .... | 7 30 | 8 0 | 8 30 | 9 0 | 9 20 | 9 40 | 9 57 | .... | 10 35 | 10 57 | 11 15 | | 5 35 | 5 55 | 6 15 | .... | 6 35 |
| Thanet Road | .... | 7 38 | 8 8 | 8 38 | 9 8 | 9 30 | 9 48 | 10 5 | .... | 10 45 | 11 7 | 11 25 | | 5 45 | 5 6 | 25 6 35 | 6 45 | .... |
| Broadstairs Front | .... | 7 48 | 8 18 | 8 48 | 9 18 | 9 40 | 9 58 | 10 15 | .... | 10 55 | 11 17 | 11 35 | | 5 55 | 6 15 | 6 35 | 6 45 | 6 55 |
| Broadstairs Station | .... | 7 53 | 8 23 | 8 53 | 9 23 | 9 45 | 10 3 | 10 20 | .... | 11 0 | 11 22 | 11 40 | | 6 0 | 6 20 | 6 40 | 6 50 | 7 0 |
| Tramway Depot | 7 30 | 7 58 | 8 28 | 8 58 | 9 28 | 9 50 | 10 8 | 10 25 | 10 45 | 11 5 | 11 28 | 11 45 | | 6 5 | 6 25 | 6 45 | 6 55 | 7 5 |
| Northdown Corner | 7 37 | 8 5 | 8 35 | 9 5 | 9 35 | 9 58 | 10 15 | 10 32 | 10 52 | 11 12 | 11 36 | 11 52 | | 6 12 | 6 32 | .... | .... | .... |
| Athelstan Road (Top) | 7 42 | 8 11 | 8 41 | 9 11 | 9 41 | 10 4 | 10 22 | 10 38 | 10 58 | 11 18 | 11 42 | 11 58 | | 6 18 | 6 38 | .... | .... | .... |
| Margate Harbour | 7 48 | 8 17 | 8 47 | 9 17 | 9 47 | 10 10 | 10 27 | 10 45 | 11 5 | 11 26 | 11 48 | 12 6 | | 6 26 | 6 46 | .... | .... | .... |
| Margate Station | 7 53 | 8 22 | 8 52 | 9 22 | 9 52 | 10 14 | 10 32 | 10 52 | 11 12 | 11 32 | 11 53 | 12 12 | | 6 32 | .... | .... | .... | .... |
| Westbrook .... arr | 7 58 | 8 28 | 8 58 | 9 28 | 9 58 | 10 18 | 10 36 | 10 58 | 11 18 | 11 38 | 11 58 | 12 18 | | 6 38 | .... | .... | .... | .... |

| | A | A | A | C | C | | | | | | | | | | |
|---|---|---|---|---|---|---|---|---|---|---|---|---|---|---|---|
| Westbrook .... dep. | .... | .... | 8 0 | 8 30 | 9 0 | 9 20 | 10 0 | | 5 20 | 5 40 | 6 0 | 6 20 | .... | 6 40 | |
| Margate Station | .... | .... | 8 5 | 8 35 | 9 5 | 9 35 | 10 5 | | 5 25 | 5 45 | 6 5 | 6 25 | .... | 6 45 | |
| Margate Harbour | .... | .... | 8 10 | 8 40 | 9 12 | 9 42 | 10 12 | | 5 32 | 5 52 | 6 12 | 6 32 | 6 46 | 6 52 | |
| Athelstan Road (Top) | .... | .... | 8 16 | 8 46 | 9 20 | 9 50 | 10 20 | | 5 40 | 6 0 | 6 20 | 6 40 | 6 52 | 7 0 | |
| Northdown Corner | .... | .... | 8 22 | 8 52 | 9 27 | 9 57 | 10 27 | | 5 47 | 6 7 | 6 27 | 6 47 | 6 58 | 7 7 | |
| Tramway Depot | 7 30 | 8 0 | 8 30 | 9 0 | 9 35 | 10 5 | 10 35 | | 5 55 | 6 15 | 6 35 | 6 55 | 7 5 | 7 15 | |
| Broadstairs Station | 7 35 | 8 5 | 8 35 | 9 5 | 9 40 | 10 10 | 10 40 | | 6 0 | 6 20 | 6 40 | 7 0 | .... | .... | |
| Broadstairs Front | 7 40 | 8 10 | 8 40 | 9 10 | 9 45 | 10 15 | 10 45 | | 6 5 | 6 25 | .... | .... | .... | .... | |
| Thanet Road | 7 50 | 8 20 | 8 50 | 9 20 | 9 55 | 10 25 | 10 55 | | 6 15 | 6 35 | .... | .... | .... | .... | |
| Ramsgate Harbour | 7 58 | 8 28 | 8 58 | 9 30 | 10 5 | 10 32 | 11 5 | | 6 25 | .... | .... | .... | .... | .... | |
| Ramsgate S. E. Station | .... | .... | .... | 9 43 | 10 18 | 10 43 | 11 18 | | 6 38 | .... | .... | .... | .... | .... | |

DAILY.

Thence every 30 mins. until

A Not on Sundays.

B Not on Sundays between Ramsgate and Depot.

C Not on Sundays between Margate and Depot.

27.　　On Elthelbert Terrace, car 32 waits to use the interlaced track. One can only speculate that "gauntlet" tracks were employed at this location to save the cost of installing two sets of points. (H.Nicol/National Tramway Museum)

## Isle of Thanet Electric Tramways.

Top Road Service.—Broadstairs and Ramsgate (via Gladstone Road).

| | | C | C | C | | | | | |
|---|---|---|---|---|---|---|---|---|---|
| **TO RAMSGATE** | Tramway Depot .. | 7 10 | 8 10 | .. | | | Thence | | 6 0 |
| | Church St., St. Peter's | 7 11 | 8 11 | .. | | | every 40 | | .. |
| | Broadstairs Station .. | 7 15 | 8 15 | 9 20 10 25 | 2 0 | | minutes | | 6 3 |
| | Bromstone Corner .. | 7 18 | 8 23 | 9 23 10 28 | 2 3 | | until | | .. |
| | Thanet Road .. .. | 7 23 | 8 30 | 9 29 10 35 | 2 10 | | | | 6 10 |
| | Ramsgate Harbour .. | 7 28 | 8 40 | 9 37 10 45 | 2 18 | | | | 6 18 |
| | Ramsgate S. E. Station | .. | 8 55 | .. | | | | | |

| | | | | | 9 | | |
|---|---|---|---|---|---|---|---|
| **TO BROADSTAIRS** | Ramsgate S. E. Station | .. | | | 6 50 | .. | *Leaves S. E. |
| | Ramsgate Harbour ..| 2 20 | Thence | | 7 0 | .. | Station at 6.40 |
| | Thanet Road .. .. | 2 28 | every 40 | | 7 8 | .. | and runs |
| | Bromstone Corner .. | 2 35 | minutes | | .. | .. | through to |
| | Broadstairs Station .. | 2 38 | until | | 7 10 | .. | Depot. |
| | Church St., St. Peter's | .. | | | .. | .. | |
| | Tramway Depot .. | .. | | | .. | .. | |

C Not on Sundays.

### Early Closing & Market Days

| | Early Clo. | Market |
|---|---|---|
| Birchington .. | Thurs. | .. |
| Broadstairs .. | Thurs. | .. |
| Canterbury .. | Thurs. | .. Sat. and altern. Mon. |
| Deal .. | Thurs. | .. |
| Dover .. | Wed. | .. Sat. |
| Faversham .. | Thurs. | ..Wed. and Sat. |
| Folkestone .. | Wed. | .. |
| Herne Bay .. | Thurs. | .. |
| Margate .. | Thurs. | .. Sat. |
| Ramsgate .. | Thurs. | .. |
| Sandwich .. | Thurs. | ..Wed. and altern. Mon. |
| Whitstable .. | Wed. | .. |

28.   One of the "narrow" (41-50 batch) cars waits at the foot of Athelstan Road for Margate bound car 54 to clear the single track.  (FJ)

29.   We now reverse the viewing point from the previous photograph. This picture probably dates from the first summer of tramway operation along Athelstan Road.

30.    Car 22 traverses the single track in Alexandra Road at the corner of St.Paul's Church by Arthur Road.

31.    The flags are out and the youth of the district ensconced on the top deck of car 7 seem to be having a rare old time. In the meantime, car 19 sidles past on the loop outside St.Paul's Church. Was this a Sunday School outing or a treat for a group of London kids whose families may have been too poor to send them on a seaside holiday? Whatever the cause for the celebration, one suspects the conductor will soon have to pour cold water on the high jinks when he points out that those flags are being waved dangerously near the 500 volt overhead wires. (C.Carter)

32.    Car 54 is depicted on the single track in Northdown Road. (FJ)

33.    We can note the elegant bracket arm at the corner of Sweyn Road and Northdown Road. One of the "narrow" trams, in this case car 43, approaches the photographer. (FJ)

34.    Car 7 loads in Northdown Road. On the opposite track, car 33 is still showing signs of First World War neglect, and from the look of it, it is in need of a complete overhaul and repaint. Some trams during the 1914-1918 period received a sage green livery instead of the usual crimson red and white. (FJ)

35.     The tracks in this part of Northdown Road were laid close together, thus it was impossible for two trams to pass each other safely. As it is, the oncoming motorist seems to have left just enough room to squeeze past car 31.  (FJ)

───────────►

36.     On a gloomy day we encounter car 26 nearing the end of its working life. This view is taken from the corner of Harold Road and Northdown Road. One can note with scepticism the tram scrappers' argument that railbound vehicles interfered with other traffic – even in 1936-37 this tram has the road to itself. (R.Elliott)

───────────►

37.     Just before the first section of private right of way is reached, cars 31 and 51 pass at a spot where today Northdown Road is joined by Devonshire Gardens. However, in this 1920s scene this is all open countryside.  (FJ)

38.     We look from the beginning of the reserved track in a westerly direction towards Cliftonville. This was obviously not high season as only two passengers are sampling the delights of top deck travel on car 58.  (FJ)

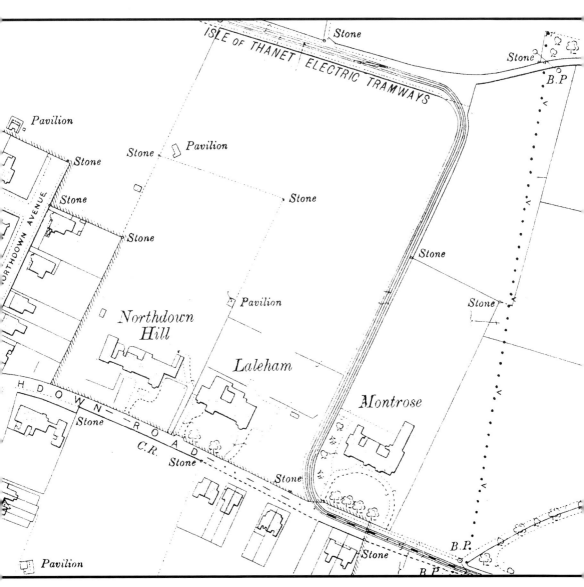

39.     The sign by the TEAS & ICES hut proclaims PRIVATE ROAD as a discouragement for unwitting motorists tempted to take a short cut along the tramlines. Car 45 is shown before its conversion to single deck, one man operation.  (FJ)

40.　　On 9th December 1928, car 22 passes the shuttered refreshment hut. Note the poster for the DREAMLAND SUPER CINEMA in Margate. (H.Nicol/National Tramway Museum)

41.    The private right of way used to connect Northdown Road with Lower Northdown Road. After the demise of the trams this stretch of track became a public footpath. (R.Elliott)

42.    Car 58 has just emerged from the reserved track into Lower Northdown Road. The grounds of Montrose are on the left and the entrance to Surrey House is on the left (FJ)

44.    All Thanet trams were equipped with swivel head trolleys, which allowed a good deal of lateral movement. This is demonstrated in this picture of car 33 by the entrance to Laleham Road. The use of this type of trolley head meant that overhead wires did not have to hang centrally over the track and, as seen here, they could be attached to bracket arms on one side of the road. (FJ)

43.    A few yards on from the previous view we catch up with car 19 making its way towards Cliftonville. (FJ)

45.	Trams in this part of Thanet had the country lanes to themselves, and passengers on car 38 can appreciate the trees swaying in the breeze and the wind rippling the neighbouring cornfields.

46.	This card was sent on 11th September 1905, and shows car 2 just past Ivy Cottages, with the Wheat Sheaf public house on the left.

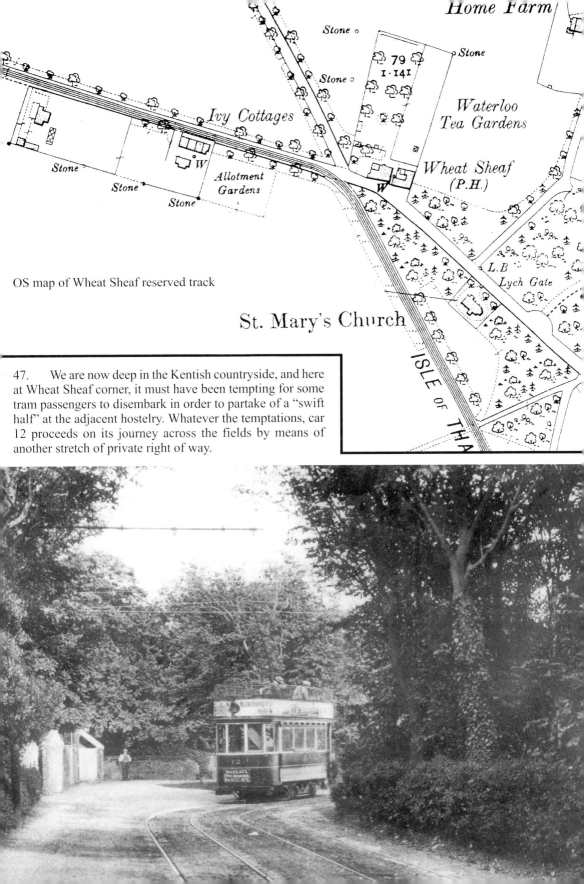

Stone

Home Farm

Stone

Stone

79
1·141

Stone

Waterloo
Tea Gardens

Ivy Cottages

W

Wheat Sheaf
(P.H.)

Stone

Allotment
Gardens

Stone

Stone

W

L.B
Lych Gate

St. Mary's Church

OS map of Wheat Sheaf reserved track

ISLE OF THA

47.    We are now deep in the Kentish countryside, and here at Wheat Sheaf corner, it must have been tempting for some tram passengers to disembark in order to partake of a "swift half" at the adjacent hostelry. Whatever the temptations, car 12 proceeds on its journey across the fields by means of another stretch of private right of way.

48.     At this lovely location we tarry awhile just to watch the trams go by. First up is car 8 whose bright new livery sparkles in the sunshine. (FJ)

49.    Next along is car 20 which looks decidedly shabby compared to its sister vehicle. In the shade of the trees a crowd of would be passengers struggles to come to terms with the fact that there is precious little room on this particular tramcar.  (FJ)

50.    The reserved track used to link the Wheat Sheaf with Green Lane and Northdown Hill. Part of it has now become a footpath, but housing and new roads have spoilt the bucolic atmosphere of this scene of bygone tranquillity.  (FJ)

51.    Car 18 ascends Northdown Hill. The double tracks here by Victoria Avenue were offset towards the eastern side of the highway. (FJ)

52.     Standing out against the skyline, car 47 rounds the bend from Westover Road to Northdown Hill. The points and connecting track to St.Peters Depot are in the foreground.  (FJ)

53.     Midday outside the depot and car 14 is just about to take up service.  (FJ)

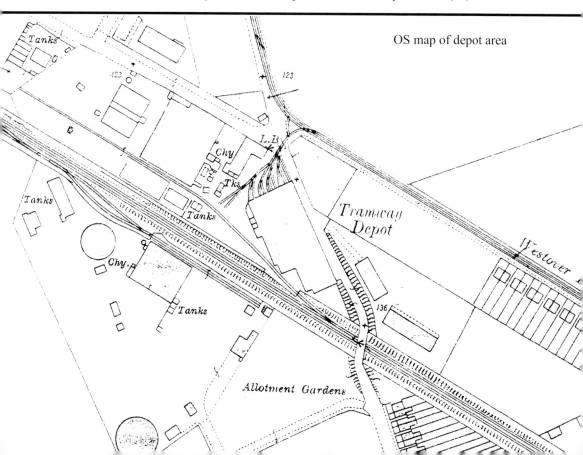

OS map of depot area

54.    Further evidence of the desolate nature of the area surrounding the depot is supplied by this view of car 59. Note the destination board affixed to the side rocker panel above the truck. (C.Carter)

55.    Car 50 exhibits one of the early "homemade" windscreens. This vehicle has been drafted in for a spell on permanent way duty. It is towing the four wheel PW truck. (FJ)

56.    This is a classic shot of one of the "narrow" cars. Clearly visible is the circle excised from the top deck advertising, which betrays the former location of the headlamp. (FJ)

57.    Car 45 stands on the entrance tracks to St.Peters Depot. Note the shield at the base of the trolley pole. This device was intended to prevent ingress of rainwater to the trolley standard. (FJ)

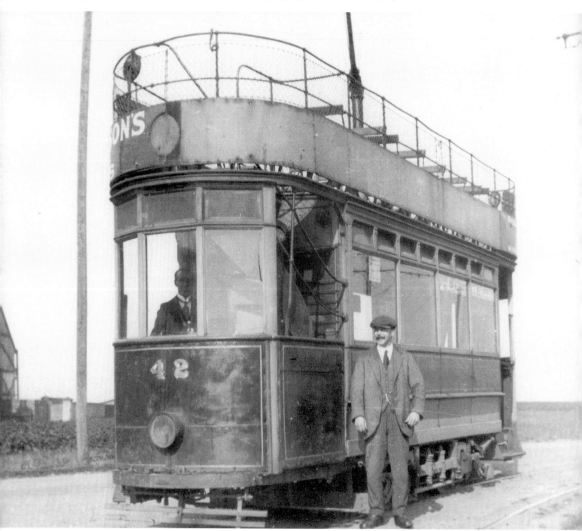

58.    St.Peters Depot is seen out of season with a number of cars under cover. During the summer months the shed would be almost empty with every available tram out on the road. In those days "health & safety" was very much down to the individual, thus the maintenance pits between the rails inside the depot are completely open to a painfully unauthorised inspection! (H.Nicol/National Tramway Museum)

←

59.     Before we enter for a good look round, we pause to observe some members of the company's workforce together with cars 22, 3 and 12. This view dates from the 1920s.  (FJ)

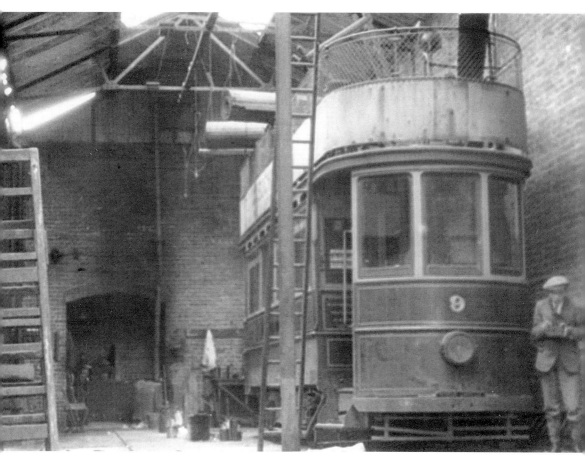

←

60.     After the First World War the maintenance arrears were tackled with a will. The latest car to be renovated is no.11, which stands ready for service. (FJ)

61.     Unfortunately, the identity of the young man with the camera remains a mystery, as does the nature of the rolls of material resting on the top deck rails. In the left background a small forge enabled the tramway blacksmith to effect some simple repairs to trucks and handrails. (FJ)

62.    Car 52 is next on the rebuilding list and the block and tackle awaits the foreman and his mate. For obvious reasons, most of the renovation of the bodywork and electric apparatus occurred in wintertime.  (FJ)

| 37S 8984 | | |
|---|---|---|
| THE ISLE OF THANET | | |
| ELECTRIC SUPPLY Co., LTD. | | |
| UP | FARE | DOWN |
| 1 | 1D | 16 |
| 2 | | 15 |
| 3 | | 14 |
| 4 | | 13 |
| 5 | | 12 |
| 6 | | 11 |
| 7 | TICKET TO BE SHOWN ON DEMAND. | 10 |
| 8 | | 9 |
| 9 | | 8 |
| 10 | | 7 |
| 11 | | 6 |
| 12 | | 5 |
| 13 | | 4 |
| 14 | | 3 |
| 15 | | 2 |
| 16 | | 1 |

For Stage Numbers See Fare Bills.

For Stage Numbers See Fare Bills.

Bell Punch Co. Uxbridge. 11-71

63.    The body of car 36 has been jacked on to four handily placed barrels and the truck has been disconnected and removed for stripping down and cleaning. The carriage builder pictured here already has a stack of seasoned timber to aid his next job, which will be the repanelling of this tramcar. He has already started work on the vehicle on the right. (FJ)

64.    Top deck panels were hoisted away from the lower saloon and were tied to the depot roof, whilst work could continue on replacing rotten and worn flooring. In the days before acrylic paints and sealants, the job of making everything waterproof had to be a thorough one.  (FJ)

65.    In the centre of the picture a lower saloon from one of the 21-40 batch of cars has had its platforms and staircases removed. Inside the lower saloon work is proceeding apace to replace the lower deck bench seating.  (FJ)

66.    In the late 1920s and early 1930s the company settled on its final form of driver's windscreen. Some trams had sported no less than three different styles during their lifetimes. The craftsman depicted here shows us how it was done with a solid example of depot carpentry.  (FJ)

67.    Car 54 also appears on the cover of this book. Repairs are taking place to its lifeguard and tray, which were fixed just below the fender and in front of the running wheels. Should any hapless pedestrian fall in front of the tram, then the lifeguard gate would be tripped and the tray lowered to scoop up the unlucky victim. In theory, serious or fatal injuries would thereby be avoided. Needless to say, the replacing buses did not have these safety features.  (FJ)

68.     We take our leave of the depot with this scene of the assembled staff. During the First World War female staff were employed to cover for men who had been called to the colours. Morale amongst the company's tramway workers was always said to be high.

69.     Westover Road was originally a tram only private right of way. Over the years this status had been eroded by speculative house builders. Car 47 has been caught on film shortly after a summer shower. Most of the company's private roads were later incorporated into public thoroughfares. (FJ)

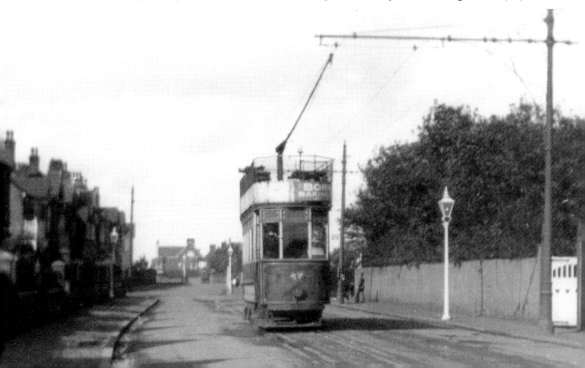

70.    We are looking south at St.Peters railway bridge. The single track here was laid on a structure, that had to be partly rebuilt and strengthened for the trams.  (FJ)

71.     The first of the fleet stands at the corner of Church Street and Albion Road. Again, there seem to be more prospective passengers than there is space available.  (FJ)

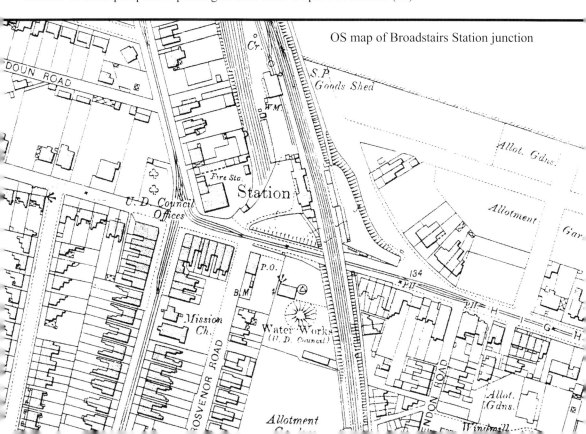

OS map of Broadstairs Station junction

72.     Car 30 is pictured at the junction of St.Peters Park Road and St.Peters Road. To the right of the car is a short section of single track. For many of the passengers the wearing of a cloche hat was obviously *de rigueur*; indeed, very few folk in those days would dream of venturing on to the streets without the correct headgear.  (H.Nicol/National Tramway Museum)

73.     The northern end of Osborne Road was the terminal point of the "Top Road" service, which skirted the back of Broadstairs before rejoining the main line to continue to Ramsgate Harbour. Traffic was light on this section and in the early 1920s the management converted car 42 (seen here) to one man operation. The staircases were removed and the entrances were reversed so that front end passenger boarding could take place, with the motorman collecting the fares and giving out the tickets. Here the driver/conductor swings the trolley in preparation for the journey to Ramsgate. The return fare was a mere four and a half old pence.  (C.Carter)

74.     We progress in time to the mid 1930s, but we remain at the same location as the previous photograph. Two man operation has now been restored to the "Top Road", as passenger loadings have risen due to new house building along the route. The wonderful summer sunshine enhances the appearance of car 2 as it waits to proceed on its way. (R.Elliott)

75. On the left of the picture is the entrance to Broadstairs Station. Car 57 has just tackled the gradient after passing under Broadstairs High Street railway bridge. (FJ)

76. No doubt the top deck passengers on car 59 have been requested by the conductor to remain seated as the tram trundles under the bridge. A warning notice fixed to the overhead structure echoes the advice given by the conductor. The trolley wire that carries the electric current has been offset to the left of the tram. (C.Carter)

77.      At the corner of High Street and Queens Road, we view a tram descending the single track in Queens Road. There were no signals and drivers relied on line of sight navigation. At times of reduced visibility an inspector, or any "volunteer" sent from the depot, would act as a human token on certain single track sections in the main line.

78.      This is Dumpton Park Drive near Dumpton Gap Road. A gloomy day in the 1930s sees car 34 heading along private right of way towards Ramsgate. After the abandonment of the trams this stretch of the route was left in a fairly primitive state, and only in the 1950s and 1960s was it brought up to public highway standards.  (FJ)

79. Car 49 halts at the parting of the ways. To the left is the embryonic Salisbury Avenue (the "Top Road" service), and straight ahead is the main line leading to Broadstairs. Centre poles have been retained because, in theory at least, motorists were banned from traversing these tram only roads. (FJ)

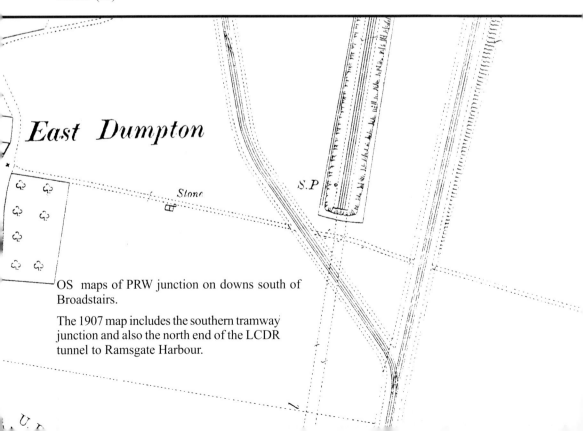

East Dumpton

Stone

S.P

OS maps of PRW junction on downs south of Broadstairs.

The 1907 map includes the southern tramway junction and also the north end of the LCDR tunnel to Ramsgate Harbour.

# RAMSGATE

80.    Architectural interest there is a-plenty in this view of colonnaded Wellington Crescent. Of course, to a tramway enthusiast the appearance of car 40 adds that bit extra to a charming scene redolent of the Edwardian era.

The 1933 edition reveals the revised junction arrangements and that the LCDR tunnel had been abandoned, following the opening of the curve linking the old routes. Part of the tunnel was used for a small electric railway, which is shown in pictures 82-87 in *Kent Narrow Gauge*.

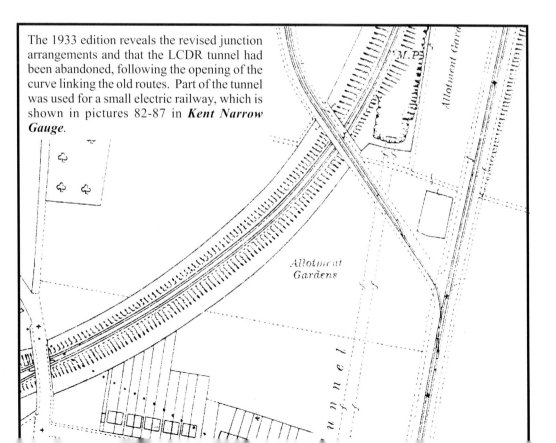

81.　　Where Wellington Crescent joins Madeira Walk an artillery piece is strategically positioned to repel any continental invaders. However, its function is very much more symbolic than practical, in contrast to car 20 which is firmly part of the work-a-day world.

82.　　Many postcard photographers have delighted in portraying the charms of Ramsgate as viewed from the ornamental rock gardens adjacent to Madeira Walk. We admire the broad sweep of the harbour and notice the solitary tramcar descending the slope to the quayside.

83.    From a similar vantage point to the previous view, we catch up with car 13. One can almost hear the application of the brakes as the car takes the bend on the down grade. The railings to the left of the car indicate the spot where car 41 took the plunge over the cliff.

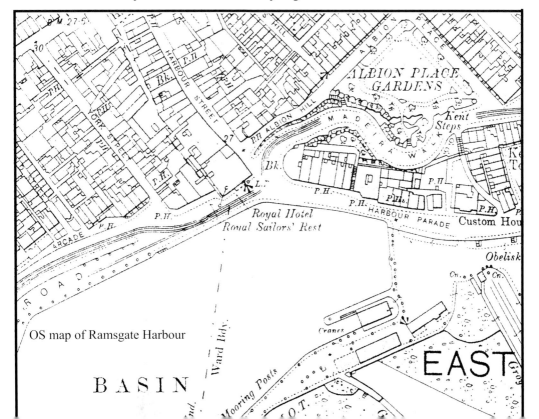

OS map of Ramsgate Harbour

84.    On 3rd August 1905, the motorman of car 41 lost control of his vehicle on Madeira Walk. The tram gathered speed, derailed and careered over the precipice. The shattered remains depicted here were deemed beyond salvage.

85.    This is the first of four pictures taken looking east along Madeira Walk. Car 55 in original condition descends the hill. The date is probably the summer of 1902.

86.    Car 34 has been equipped with top deck canopy destination boards as well as side destination boards on the rocker panels. As there were no stops on the hill, the driver of car 34 can maintain a steady momentum as he climbs the gradient.

87.     The rocky waterfalls of Albion Place Gardens provide the setting for this very rare view of bogie car 23 in "as delivered" condition. Officially, the reason for shortening these cars was the frequent occurrence of derailments when the brakes were being applied. The small "pony" wheels of each bogie truck were prone to lift and "come off the iron". This was to be regretted, because in many respects these particular trams represent the acme of elegance and style in late Victorian coachbuilding.

88.     The scene switches to the mid 1930s. Car 6 inches gingerly round the steep curves. (R.Elliott)

89.     At this location nowadays one is acutely aware of the faded glories of Ramsgate. Where once brightly coloured tramcars ran past immaculately kept gardens and small hotels, there is now, in the first decade of the twenty-first century, an air of decrepitude.  (R.Elliott)

90.     In the first few months after the opening of the line car 47 is pictured at East Cliff, Madeira Walk. This tram is working the "Top Road" service to Broadstairs.

91.    The "Reliance" wagonette has taken on a full load for the day's excursion to Canterbury. Here on the quayside an alternative form of public transport is on offer in the shape of Isle of Thanet Electric Tramways and Lighting Company car 54. This was a golden age in British travel – added to the delights portrayed in this view were the steam trains at the nearby Ramsgate Harbour Station and of course the sailing ships. Not a pollution causing internal combustion engine to be seen or smelt!

92.    Ramsgate Harbour is a veritable hive of activity in this 1901 view. The tram nearest the camera has just negotiated the harbour crossover, meanwhile in the quayside siding car 45, which has yet to receive driver's windscreens, waits to leave on the "Top Road" route. One of the original eight wheel cars is about to ascend Royal Parade.

93.    This card was sent on 22nd August 1906. At the foot of Royal Parade a Thanet tram halts to take on passengers. Other folk are content just to stroll in the sunshine and perhaps admire the splendid array of sailing vessels moored in the harbour.

94.    Was there really more time to do things in days gone past? – Or is this an illusion created by this evocative midday panorama of Ramsgate Harbour? Whatever the answer, this whole scene certainly imparts an unhurried atmosphere. People waiting for main line trams are standing nonchalantly in the roadway. Car 6 has gained several customers for the leisurely trip over the downs to Osborne Road, Broadstairs, and the local fishing fleet seems totally becalmed. Were anyone to invent time travel, one suspects this location would become a favourite holiday destination! (FJ)

95.     We are back with Dr.Nicol on 9th December 1928. The backdrop is supplied by the Admiral Harvey Inn, whilst in the foreground the conductor and motorman of car 3 plus a trio of schoolboys eye the photographer. The notice half way up the traction standard advertises the Thanet Circular Tour as operated by the tramway company's motor buses – all twenty miles (32km) for the princely sum of one shilling and sixpence! (H.Nicol/National Tramway Museum)

96.     The younger element of the audience seems to have lost interest, but the conductor has been persuaded to make one last pose before the tram heads off up Royal Parade. (H.Nicol/National Tramway Museum)

97.     The famous French postcard firm of Louis Levy included this picture of car 16 in its range. The carriageway and the well proportioned arches lead the eye effortlessly round the western end of the harbour. In the opinion of many this architectural sweep is one of the most pleasing of any seaside resort.

98.    Nelson Crescent intersects with Royal Parade at the beginning of the Paragon Promenade. Car 23 starts its downward journey to the harbour. Note that the double track is laid very close to kerb.

99.    Car 27 is pictured in St.Augustines Road at the gates of The Grange. Behind the tram is the tower of St.Augustine's RC Church, that was designed by E.Welby Pugin.

100.    There was a short section of reserved track leading to the old South Eastern Railway Company's Ramsgate Town Station. Car 11 is nearing journey's end as it passes car 1 which is returning to Margate. (FJ)

OS map of Ramsgate terminus

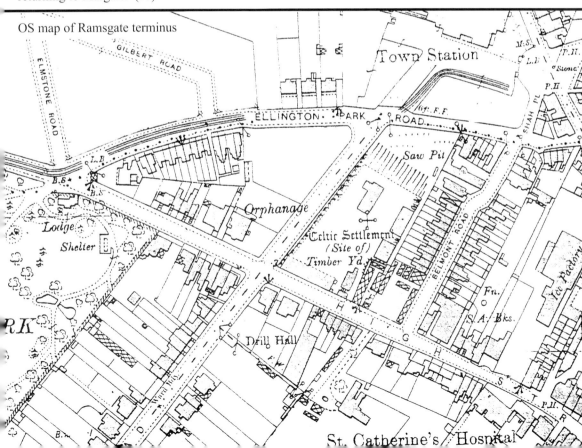

101.    After the Southern Railway closed Ramsgate Town Station in 1926, the tramway company complained bitterly that their main traffic objective had been removed almost overnight. The old station buildings were then demolished and the site was left semi derelict. Unfortunately, finances did not permit a tramway extension to the new railway station, which was constructed to the north of the High Street.

# ROLLING STOCK

102. This is a broadside view of a member of the 1-20 batch of cars, which were supplied by the American St.Louis Car Company in 1901. This vehicle has lost its original plate frame truck.

103. Car 10 is pictured in near original condition, except for the headlamp, which has been removed from the upper deck canopy. The St.Louis frame trucks were said to be very durable and hard riding. This latter feature probably convinced the tramway company to invest in more modern trucks, which gave a better ride for the passengers. (FJ)

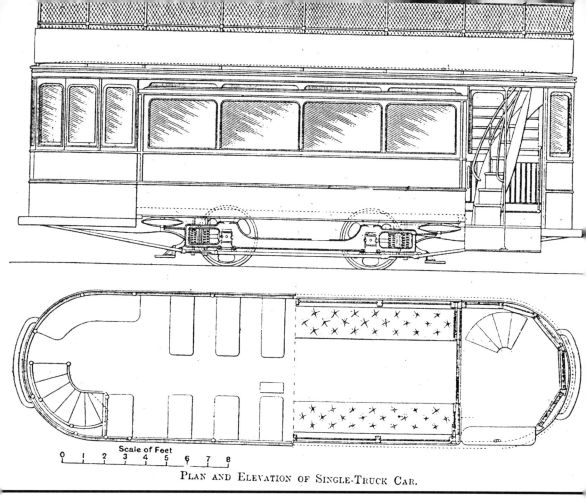

Scale of Feet
0  1  2  3  4  5  6  7  8

PLAN AND ELEVATION OF SINGLE-TRUCK CAR.

Plan of one of the 1-20 series cars.

104. Car 6 has been decommissioned from revenue service and is now acting as a tool car for the permanent way workers. A wheelbarrow full of wooden paving blocks has just been transferred to the interior of the tram. (FJ)

105. The eight wheel, bogie cars supplied by St.Louis in 1901 were handsome vehicles which had the potential of transporting large crowds of holidaymakers. However, the reversed (i.e. pony wheel forward) maximum traction trucks were vulnerable to derailments. This illustration shows car 22 on a test run in the winter of 1900/01.

106. Car 35 is travelling down Madeira Walk, Ramsgate. It has received destination boards and a partial set of adverts, but does not appear to possess lifeguard gates. This batch was numbered 21-40.

107.    Every tram in this batch was soon withdrawn from service. Drastic treatment was applied to the bodywork, which was shortened to a four and a half window bay configuration. A four wheel, single truck replaced the unreliable maximum traction bogies. Car 26 is depicted in rebuilt state some time in the 1920s.  (FJ)

108.   This 1922 view of car 40 was taken by George Gundry on the forecourt of Ramsgate Town Station. In an interview with the author, George related that the fleet was well maintained and that car 40, on which he rode to Ramsgate Harbour, had a fair turn of speed. He further recalled that the first motormen employed by the company were very wary of applying too much pressure to the brakes on the original bogie cars. Much trouble was experienced by derailments after the brakes had been used. A derailment could mean loss of earnings for the motorman or, in extreme cases, dismissal from the job.  (G.L.Gundry)

109.    Trams numbered 41-50 were constructed by G.F.Milnes & Co of Hadley, Shropshire. They were delivered in 1901 and were characterised by their narrow (6ft. 3ins/1905mm) width. They were quickly equipped with driver's windscreens and, as seen here in this view of car 42, were soon at work amongst the rest of the fleet.  (FJ)

**24C 3401**

THE ISLE OF THANET
ELECTRIC SUPPLY CO., LTD.
MOTOR SERVICE

UP     FARE

**2d**

For Stage No. see Fare Bill.

Ticket to be shown on demand.

For Stage No. see Fare Bill.

110.    In the 1920s car 42 was altered for one man operation on the "Top Road" service. As we can observe in this picture, the stairs have been removed and the entrances transposed so that passengers can board directly by the motorman. The seats on the top deck have no apparent value as they can now be reached solely by the use of a ladder! Note the standard Brill 21E truck of six feet/1829mm wheelbase, which was used worldwide and was one of the most successful engineering applications of its type.

111.    Car 43 shows some variations in livery details especially in the top panels of the driver's windscreen. (FJ)

112.    Car 45 was converted to single deck, front entrance operation for use on the "Top Road". Here it is pictured outside St.Peters Depot on trackwork duties with the PW Department. Several apocryphal stories are told of car 45 being driven at 50mph/80km/h along Salisbury Avenue, Broadstairs, when racing across the downs in the direction of Ramsgate Harbour. It seems a certain Bill Tattersall was the star of these "flying motorman" exploits, and several passengers of a nervous disposition had to be comforted after their unwilling participation in these early speed trials! (FJ)

113. Car 48 still possesses one of the original "homemade" windscreens. One can also observe the reversed staircases, which were a feature of the Thanet fleet. These were frowned upon by most tramway operators as they were considered to impede the all round vision of the driver. (FJ)

114. Fleet numbers 51-60 were allocated to trams built in 1903 by the British Electric Car Company of Trafford Park. This manufacturer is generally regarded as having supplied a somewhat less than robust product, but the Thanet cars were well maintained by the depot staff and shortcomings of construction were not allowed to surface. In this photo car 52 is being given a thorough overhaul, which includes new vestibules. (FJ)

115.  Car 58 has been fitted with an early three window windscreen. Note that Heinz 57 Varieties were as popular in the 1920s as they are now.  (FJ)

116.    Car 58 reappears after having been spruced up by the depot craftsmen. Various minor livery changes can be noted, as well as the replacement of the top deck canopy panel.  (FJ)

117.    Yet another windscreen variation – this time a double window with half drop has been supplied to car 57.  (FJ)

118.  Photos of the interior of Thanet trams are very rare. We glance into the lower saloon of car 53, which is depicted in its final state shortly before withdrawal from service.  (FJ)

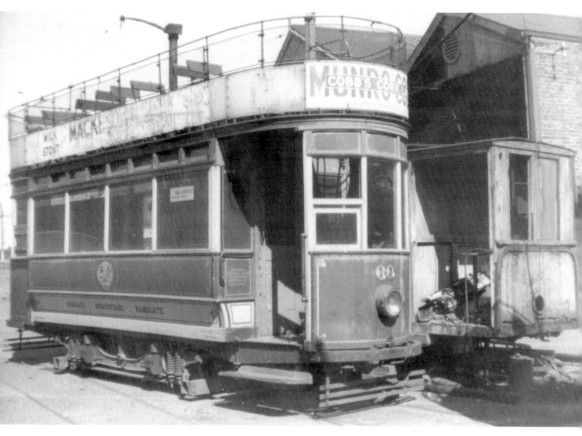

119.    It finally remains to describe cars 60 and 61. Car 60 had its original Brill 21E truck swapped for a St.Louis cast frame one. Car 61, seen in derelict state on the right of the picture, was a works car equipped with a Brush Aa type truck.  (FJ)

# FINALE

120. The entrance tracks to Westbrook Depot stand as mute witness to the past glories of the Thanet tramway system. Although the old trams took their leave on the evening of Wednesday, 27th March 1937, a new generation of "congestion busting" tramcars could supply quality transport to local residents, and could aid in the economic regeneration of the area.

# Middleton Press

Easebourne Lane, Midhurst, W Sussex. GU29 9AZ Tel: 01730 813169 Fax: 01730 812601
*If books are not available from your local transport stockist, order direct with cheque,
Visa or Mastercard, post free UK.*

## BRANCH LINES
Branch Line to Allhallows
Branch Line to Alton
Branch Lines around Ascot
Branch Line to Ashburton
Branch Lines around Bodmin
Branch Line to Bude
Branch Lines around Canterbury
Branch Lines around Chard & Yeovil
Branch Lines around Cromer
Branch Lines to East Grinstead
Branch Lines of East London
Branch Lines to Effingham Junction
Branch Lines around Exmouth
Branch Line to Fairford
Branch Lines around Gosport
Branch Line to Hawkhurst
Branch Lines to Horsham
Branch Lines around Huntingdon
Branch Line to Ilfracombe
Branch Line to Kingswear
Branch Lines to Launceston & Princetown
Branch Lines to Longmoor
Branch Line to Looe
Branch Line to Lyme Regis
Branch Lines around March
Branch Lines around Midhurst
Branch Line to Minehead
Branch Line to Moretonhampstead
Branch Line to Padstow
Branch Lines around Plymouth
Branch Lines to Seaton and Sidmouth
Branch Line to Selsey
Branch Lines around Sheerness
Branch Line to Shrewsbury
Branch Line to Swanage *updated*
Branch Line to Tenterden
Branch Lines around Tiverton
Branch Lines to Torrington
Branch Lines to Tunbridge Wells
Branch Line to Upwell
Branch Lines of West London
Branch Lines around Weymouth
Branch Lines around Wisbech

## NARROW GAUGE
Branch Line to Lynton
Branch Lines around Portmadoc 1923-46
Branch Lines around Porthmadog 1954-94
Branch Line to Southwold
Douglas to Port Erin
Kent Narrow Gauge
Two-Foot Gauge Survivors
Romneyrail
Southern France Narrow Gauge
Vivarais Narrow Gauge

## SOUTH COAST RAILWAYS
Ashford to Dover
Bournemouth to Weymouth
Brighton to Eastbourne
Brighton to Worthing
Dover to Ramsgate
Eastbourne to Hastings
Hastings to Ashford
Portsmouth to Southampton
Southampton to Bournemouth

## SOUTHERN MAIN LINES
Basingstoke to Salisbury
Bromley South to Rochester
Crawley to Littlehampton
Dartford to Sittingbourne
East Croydon to Three Bridges
Epsom to Horsham
Exeter to Barnstaple
Exeter to Tavistock
Faversham to Dover

London Bridge to East Croydon
Orpington to Tonbridge
Tonbridge to Hastings
Salisbury to Yeovil
Swanley to Ashford
Tavistock to Plymouth
Victoria to East Croydon
Waterloo to Windsor
Waterloo to Woking
Woking to Portsmouth
Woking to Southampton
Yeovil to Exeter

## EASTERN MAIN LINES
Fenchurch Street to Barking
Ipswich to Saxmundham
Liverpool Street to Ilford

## WESTERN MAIN LINES
Ealing to Slough
Ely to Kings Lynn
Exeter to Newton Abbot
Newton Abbot to Plymouth
Paddington to Ealing
Slough to Newbury

## COUNTRY RAILWAY ROUTES
Andover to Southampton
Bath Green Park to Bristol
Bath to Evercreech Junction
Bournemouth to Evercreech Jn.
Cheltenham to Andover
Croydon to East Grinstead
Didcot to Winchester
East Kent Light Railway
Fareham to Salisbury
Frome to Bristol
Guildford to Redhill
Reading to Basingstoke
Reading to Guildford
Redhill to Ashford
Salisbury to Westbury
Stratford upon Avon to Cheltenham
Strood to Paddock Wood
Taunton to Barnstaple
Wenford Bridge to Fowey
Westbury to Bath
Woking to Alton
Yeovil to Dorchester

## GREAT RAILWAY ERAS
Ashford from Steam to Eurostar
Clapham Junction 50 years of change
Festiniog in the Fifties
Festiniog in the Sixties
Isle of Wight Lines 50 years of change
Railways to Victory 1944-46
SECR Centenary album
Talyllyn 50 years of change
Yeovil 50 years of change

## LONDON SUBURBAN RAILWAYS
Caterham and Tattenham Corner
Charing Cross to Dartford
Clapham Jn. to Beckenham Jn.
Crystal Palace (HL) & Catford Loop
East London Line
Finsbury Park to Alexandra Palace
Kingston and Hounslow Loops
Lewisham to Dartford
Lines around Wimbledon
London Bridge to Addiscombe
Mitcham Junction Lines
North London Line
South London Line
West Croydon to Epsom
West London Line
Willesden Junction to Richmond

*London Suburban Railway continued .....*
Wimbledon to Beckenham
Wimbledon to Epsom

## STEAMING THROUGH
Steaming through Cornwall
Steaming through the Isle of Wight
Steaming through Kent
Steaming through West Hants
Steaming through West Sussex

## TRAMWAY CLASSICS
Aldgate & Stepney Tramways
Barnet & Finchley Tramways
Bath Tramways
Bournemouth & Poole Tramways
Brighton's Tramways
Burton & Ashby Tramways
Camberwell & W.Norwood Tramways
Clapham & Streatham Tramways
Croydon's Tramways
Dover's Tramways
East Ham & West Ham Tramways
Edgware and Willesden Tramways
Eltham & Woolwich Tramways
Embankment & Waterloo Tramways
Enfield & Wood Green Tramways
Exeter & Taunton Tramways
Greenwich & Dartford Tramways
Hammersmith & Hounslow Tramways
Hampstead & Highgate Tramways
Hastings Tramways
Holborn & Finsbury Tramways
Ilford & Barking Tramways
Kingston & Wimbledon Tramways
Lewisham & Catford Tramways
Liverpool Tramways 1. Eastern Routes
Liverpool Tramways 2. Southern Routes
Liverpool Tramways 3. Northern Routes
Maidstone & Chatham Tramways
Margate to Ramsgate
North Kent Tramways
Norwich Tramways
Portsmouth's Tramways
Reading Tramways
Seaton & Eastbourne Tramways
Shepherds Bush & Uxbridge Tramway
Southampton Tramways
Southend-on-sea Tramways
Southwark & Deptford Tramways
Stamford Hill Tramways
Twickenham & Kingston Tramways
Victoria & Lambeth Tramways
Waltham Cross & Edmonton Tramway
Walthamstow & Leyton Tramways
Wandsworth & Battersea Tramways

## TROLLEYBUS CLASSICS
Croydon Trolleybuses
Bournemouth Trolleybuses
Hastings Trolleybuses
Maidstone Trolleybuses
Reading Trolleybuses
Woolwich & Dartford Trolleybuses

## WATERWAY ALBUMS
Kent and East Sussex Waterways
London to Portsmouth Waterway
West Sussex Waterways

## MILITARY BOOKS
Battle over Portsmouth
Battle over Sussex 1940
Bombers over Sussex 1943-45
Bognor at War
Military Defence of West Sussex
Military Signals from the South Coast
Secret Sussex Resistance
Surrey Home Guard
Sussex Home Guard

## OTHER RAILWAY BOOKS
Garraway Father & Son
Index to all Middleton Press stations
Industrial Railways of the South-East
South Eastern & Chatham Railways
London Chatham & Dover Railway
War on the Line (SR 1939-45)